Roy and Royal

by Tom Sato
illustrated by Angela Adams

Core Decodable 101

I0806548

McGraw Hill Education

Bothell, WA • Chicago, IL • Columbus, OH • New York, NY

MHEonline.com

Send all inquiries to:
McGraw-Hill Education
8787 Orion Place
Columbus, OH 43240

ISBN: 978-0-02-145615-4
MHID: 0-02-145615-1

Printed in the United States of America.

9 10 11 12 KOD 24

Roy dug in the soil. His dog, Royal, joined him. Roy enjoyed gardening. Royal enjoyed digging.

Roy dropped seeds in the soil. He planted green beans. Royal planted a bone.

Roy used a hose. He kept the soil moist.
Roy waited for the seeds to grow.

Roy felt joy. Green points stuck out of the soil. His green beans were growing.

The green beans grew. Rabbits tried to destroy them. But Royal spoiled the rabbits' snack. He chased them away.

Roy picked his beans. Royal dug up his bone.

That night, the boy enjoyed a good dinner. Royal enjoyed his bone.